THE DEVIL SAYS MAYBE I LIKE IT

WENDY BOURGEOIS is a poet and writer. In addition to the essays she writes for her regular column in *Propeller*, her poems have appeared in *Cirque*, *Portland Review*, and other small press journals. She is a writing instructor at Portland Community College and Portland State University. This is her first book.

DANEEN BERGLAND is a poet and writer whose work has appeared in several journals, including *Propeller*, *The Cincinnati Review*, and *Hunger Mountain*, and was included in the anthology *Alive at the Center: Contemporary Poems from the Pacific Northwest*. The recipient of a writer's fellowship for poetry from Oregon Literary Arts, she is a faculty member at Portland State University.

The Devil Says Maybe I Like It

Essays on Poetry

Wendy Bourgeois

PROPELLER BOOKS

PORTLAND, OREGON • UNITED STATES OF AMERICA

First U.S. Edition, 2018

Cover and interior design by Context

Published by Propeller Books, Portland, Oregon.
ISBN 978-0-98277-047-4

www.propellerbooks.com

CONTENTS

Foreword

The other day, Wendy and I were walking her Boston terrier when I commented on the dreary façade of a house nestled among the fetching, remodeled bungalows and newly-constructed, oversized luxury-boxes looming over them in her gentrifying neighborhood. "Oh, that house needs some help," I said sadly, to which she replied that she prefers houses like that, the ones people pass over as lost causes too tacky to bother with. She likes to imagine what one could do with that interior, how fun it would be to enter that shabby shack expecting to be disappointed, only to discover a palace inside. What I saw as depressing and not long for this upwardly mobile world, she reckoned might hold hidden treasure. She wasn't willing to give up on it, and despite the ambivalence she indicates here about poetry and philosophy, she's not willing to give up on them, and she's going to show you why you shouldn't, either.

These essays were originally written for "Reading Lines," her regular column on the Propeller website. And though they worked great dealt out one at a time, they reach their full potential gathered here in one book, where they can play off one another, be thumbed through, and turned over in one's hands like a geode.

The conceit is that each little essay riffs or ruminates on one line of poetry. On the outside, this sounds simple, and maybe not that interesting if you're not into poetry or you've never heard of Mary Ruefle or John Ashberry. But even if you haven't read the poems referenced, know nothing about the poets, and don't give a hoot about poetry in general, you have much to gain from reading this book. You're going to want to know where she's going with all this.

These essays are dishy, spoken in the voice of a confidant, as she tucks each poet's line inside a closet of her own stories, secrets, and desires. What's astonishing is the way she can unpack an idea, a feeling, an experience, or an especially dense or opaque line of poetry so deftly and completely, as if picking apart a hopeless knot in an impossibly delicate chain. Once untangled, a truth sparkles under the beam of her bright intelligence. Illuminated, the line does not lose the contours of its complexity, paradox, or nuance. We can just better see its detail.

This book gives us what we want: short, digestible morsels. We can pick it up and put it down without losing our place. Each essay is the length of a bus ride or a dentist office wait, but they are not disposable, nor meant merely to pass the time. Like poems, they welcome re-reading. Though they reckon with literature and theory across time, the ageless themes are housed firmly in their modern context: Power, Death, Religion, Marriage, Beauty, Femininity, Motherhood, Love, God. If poetry is a distillation, these essays offer a concentrated drop of truth reconstituted in a personal and cultural moment.

We especially need books like this right now, in a time when we are presented with extreme binaries and oversimplifications. We need conversation, nuance, ineffability, complexity of thought. We readers need to, as she quotes William James, "be incorporated into the gaps between meaning." It's good for us. But these morsels aren't just health food—the syntax succulent, the diction layered, the vocabulary rich—they are nutrient-dense. They aren't arguments, they are interpretations and conversations with someone who is as confident in our ability to figure it out as hers. More than anything, this book of essays reminds us that poems don't offer themselves up on a platter: we have to bring an open mind, the willingness to wonder, to be at least a little lost, and to go along for the ride and see what we might find. This way of reading, thinking, and being is the promise and pleasure of creativity. It's hopeful. It's also a possible antidote for anxiety, and we're all feeling a bit (or a lot) of that these days. Living as we are in a twenty-four-hour news cycle, inundated by information (true, fake, bad, you name it) these essays welcome us into a fascinating conversation that leaves us smarter than we were before. Wendy hasn't given up on any of us yet.

—DANEEN BERGLAND

Ambivalent Attachment
an introduction

I started writing poems when I was ten, because everything sucked and no one listened to me. Then, I wrote poems because I got praise from grown-ups. Then, again because everything sucked and no one listened to me. Then because I wanted to make something beautiful and durable. Then because it was fun. Then because it was work. Then because I felt I owed it something, a relationship that outlived its pleasures, but one I could not part from without guilt. Then I stopped. And whenever I stop I think I won't start again, but I keep running into it, and it pisses me off.

Marianne Moore says in her *ars poetica*, "I too, dislike it" and absolutely everybody remembers that line, because absolutely everybody agrees with her. What is it about poems that inspire such hostility? No one goes around saying *Down with novels!* or *Longform journalism stinks!* They might think *It's over* or *What a shame no one reads*

Hawthorne anymore, but poetry, Jesus. The things I have heard. From English majors, even. I don't get it. It's for teenaged girls. It acts like it's so smart. I should try harder to like it. It's irrelevant. And so forth. Poetry students are no better, although their remarks tend towards slightly awed backhanded thoughts like "How am I supposed to critique this when it's just their feelings?" and "Poems can mean whatever you want them to."

Fair enough. Maybe poetry is for teenaged girls because it's so much like a teenaged girl. Thin skinned. Obscure. By turns irritating and endearing, haughty then gawky. Obsessed with aesthetics. Starved for affection. Nothing ever happens to it. Nothing it does matters yet. It's just hiding in its room, waiting for life to start. When I see clumsy or lazy prose, I feel at least some tenderness towards the writer, and empathy for the endless frustration of communication. Writing, as we say at the office, is hard. When I see clumsy or lazy poetry, though, especially when it's admired by the world at large, I feel like pouring gasoline on my bookshelf and setting it on fire like an Ayn Rand character. This, I recognize, is childish, bitter, and deeply uncool. You can't do life like that. You have to grow up. Maybe you outgrow poetry because it's nauseatingly vulnerable, and no amount of attention is ever enough.

Sometimes, when I steel myself for the hateful task of submitting my poems to literary journals, I think about all the poets I know in real life, and how beautiful they are, and how they don't know it, how they labor over these odd little flashes of magic no one reads, no one will probably ever read, and how dumb it is to even try, since everyone dislikes it anyway—and I love them so, so much. This book is for them.

—WENDY BOURGEOIS

The Devil Says Maybe I Like It

Privileges of Suffering

Tamed by Miltown, we lie on Mother's bed.
—Robert Lowell, "Man and Wife"

If you wake up at seven a.m. after an uneventful Tuesday in your own bed with this pernicious little Lowell gem about the aftermath of a hideous marital spat careening around your inner ear, despite the fact that you're divorced and sleep mostly alone, you can surmise that a) it's time for a refill, or b) the full range of human emotions you were so excited to experience from ages twelve through twenty-five actually kind of still suck.

Miltown, a sturdy mid-century barbiturate, didn't narrow Robert Lowell's emotional range enough to keep him out of mental institutions, but pharmaceuticals have improved since then. The other day, a friend said SSRI's ruin sincerity in art, because artists no longer have to suffer quite so deeply from the mental illnesses with which they have entertained us since the first caveman's tears mixed with powdered ore adorned some rock wall in France.

Okay, that's not exactly what he said. He said something thoughtful. I turned it into the sweeping over-generalization you see before you. I won't apologize; I bet Robert Lowell did it all the time.

I'm always insisting that artists as a breed manage to maintain just as much, or as little, emotional health as farmers or massage therapists, but I'm not sure I believe it. Lowell would never have gotten that bit about "mother's bed" without the couch, but who knows if the couch ever did him any good? His image does me good in those early mornings when I think of it—gives me a context for a very particular kind of sadness. That it's a boring sadness, numbed with routine and pills, sharpens the impact because I recognize it so completely that I barely even notice it's there anymore.

The older I get, the more intolerant I grow of any kind of direct mimetic representation of violence. Emotional or physical meanness, even when illuminating, makes me bone tired, and I can't take to my bed anymore—if I ever could—because people depend on me to show up and act sane. This is unfortunate, because it limits my ability to feel through art, and grow because of it. I read a lot of trash. I watch movies mostly from the Hays Code era—the ultimate advertisement for the tonic effects of repression in the creative process. It allows the pain of things to sneak up on you with a little joke or some Technicolor song and dance, and like a nurse with a good needle, you don't feel it going in until it's too late.

So yeah, maybe the culture's current designated basket cases are less full-frontal in their basket-casery because of the miracle of modern science. Not all of them of course, but I tend to recoil quicklike from any direct *Sturm und*

Drang—no Lars Von Trier, no environmental crisis documentaries. Mannered whimsy can break your heart too, maybe more when your kids have enough to eat and hot and cold running water and lots of shoes. One feels that Suffering, in the big sense, displays a gross lack of perspective.

So it makes sense then that Lowell's kind of privileged sufferers speak to me more clearly in their inside voices, because I'm trained not to tune reasonableness out, no matter how eviscerating the content, as long as the tone is measured. They remind me that safety and misery are not mutually exclusive, despite my tedious guilty conscience. Most days now I feel almost thoroughly tamed. I have cried and been self destructive in a thousand ways, checkering my past for the experience or the anecdote, but I never got much work done. Eventually, though, Mother's bed turned my bed. I try to get there early most nights, so I can wake up at seven a.m.

Excellent Posture

When I had no mother, I embraced order.
—Robert Pinsky, "Samurai Song"

I love this line so much that it lives on my fridge, though I am disorderly to the core. My yard looks like *Whatever Happened to Baby Jane* and my credit score would make my father weep. I loathe paperwork, can't remember my social security number, frequently lose the card and have to pay for another one, "forget" to schedule doctor appointments even though I prayed every night for years to the gods of adulthood to grant me health insurance that I now can't be bothered to use, and I recently turned forty.

But my house is clean. Really clean right now, because I'm having a party and avoiding scheduling a mammogram. Because somehow I still believe, against all evidence to the contrary, that if Social Services or cancer were to stop by one day unannounced, they would take one look at the perfect fan of *Tin House* magazines on my coffee table and know that I was an excellent human being and that no further investigation or karma would be necessary. Pinsky's line makes me feel a little chastised, and maybe that's why I like it so much. It makes me feel mothered.

Growing up in the seventies was wicked fun, mostly because my mom and everybody else's moms were too busy smoking pot and committing adultery to attempt anything resembling authoritarian parenting. But the experiment of permissiveness has had some far reaching aftereffects. The current model of Attachment Theory in psychology seems to suggest that both slovenliness and clean-freakishness result from poor, or "disorganized" attachment. This explains, I think, the popularity of TLC shows like *Hoarders* and *My Strange Addiction*. Some of us embrace order, and some of us throw spectacular tantrums to get the attention we missed when we were six.

Most of us probably embrace it sporadically, with saintly habits in one or two areas and varying degrees of disarray in the rest. I have a close friend since childhood who has pristine white carpet and three sons under the age of ten. She quit drinking recently, mostly because the wine stains were making her crazy. Some of us eat nothing but "clean food" while our taxes go unpaid. Some of us make our beds daily with hospital corners yet wear the same shirt for three days straight. I do a passable job managing people and relationships, but the stuff of the world, especially abstract stuff like "money" and "career," remain uncrossed from my to-do list for longer and longer periods as I get older.

It would be so awesome if some nice lady with a camera crew came over and lectured me on the virtues of multicolored file folders, because I, like everyone else, would prefer to have a mother than be one to myself. I get it that having your shit together is actually more comfy and snuggly in the long run than chaos, in the same way that sitting up straight will eventually hurt your back less than if you slouch, but my actual, non-idealized mother created mess and excitement everywhere she went, though she had excellent posture. She wouldn't know a multicolored file folder if it waltzed over and sang "Gold Dust Woman," so what chance do I have?

A Wake

That which is given to see
At any moment is the residue, shadowed
In gold or emerging into the clear bluish haze
Of uncertainty.
—John Ashbery, "The Gazing Grain"

I went with friends to see a beached baby grey whale, two days dead. Someone cut a window in its side so it wouldn't explode as it rotted, and its intestines spilled onto the sand and looked like bags of black muslin surrounded by a deep yellow frame of whale blubber. The thing was a juvenile, only twenty-five feet long, and I was thrilled to see it, because I had never been near one of those massive bodies, had never seen baleen up close. I resisted the urge to touch it, though I'm pretty sure I would have at least pressed one finger against its dense side, had I been alone. One of my friends made an altar out of soda cans and Styrofoam and the other played a mouth bow and sat on a piece of driftwood. I called them both hippies and felt little sense of occasion. I just looked.

We watched a mom wander up with her three kids, exclaiming like an energetic nurse, "Isn't this amazing?" The eldest girl mugged for the camera in front of the corpse with a gleam in her eye. That one's going to do fine in the world, I thought. The younger girl sobbed hysterically, and the boy turned away and kicked sand.

Hours later, I sat on a dune by myself, smoked a cigarette, and then mysteriously burst into tears. I had just received a text from my daughter that she was accepted to the art school she wanted to attend. She'll be out of the house at the end of summer. I imagine this would be obvious to nearly anyone else, but I was shocked I felt sad. I thought about the whale, someone's baby dead on a beach, and my own baby heading out into the ocean of the world, and it wasn't until I strung those pieces of recent experience together in my mind's eye and made a private tableau of them together with me at the center that I felt anything. It was embarrassing.

I try to make peace with the knowledge that I only assign meaning to suffering selfishly, if at all, because how could I survive otherwise? Things die all the time, especially young and fragile things. Everyone who looked at the whale that day made up their own story about what it meant, and whether it was a morality play or a lab report depends entirely on what each petty, pragmatic little self has on hand.

The act of witness, something everyone instinctively assigns importance to, turns out to be weirdly dumb. Not very smart. Silent. John Ashbery writes, "That which is given to see/ At any moment is the residue, shadowed/ In gold or emerging into the clear bluish haze/ Of uncertainty." We are given things to see by something or other, but those things lack context. They are residue—meaning, I think, that they're mere artifacts, the gunk of what already happened during some time we can't ever quite catch, shadowed in gold because feeling operates backwards, even in the uncertain present. Empathy fails me when it would do the most good, and then shows up later and catches me unprepared, minding my own business, and it feels like a stranger, because the enormity of the end of whales and childhood and all the other things ending, whether I like it or not, is just too big to swallow.

Silage

Perfume is what the flowers throw away.
—Paul Valery, "Of Colors"

Paul Valery is talking here about the idea that our visible temperament is what our essence rejects. So, you know, if I'm nice to old ladies that's because there's a hatefulness lurking around my inner subway station, too attached to the grime of my subconscious to climb the stairs into the light. And if you keep all your financial documents from the last fifteen years in specially labeled file folders next to your living will and shot records, well that's because your inner spaces resemble a cat hoarder's bathroom.

I just don't know what to do with this information.

My first impulse is to reject it. I'd prefer to think of the inner me as vanilla ice cream, the same all the way to the bottom of the carton. One can predict the behavior of vanilla ice cream with a fair amount of certainty. Tastes good. Melts easily. Will give brain freeze if rushed.

Reassuring, and unlikely to result in the late night discovery of a hidden vein of chocolate covered marshmallow peanuts. Some people are allergic to peanuts. One bite, and they keel over dead. I just don't need that kind of pressure.

On the other hand, thinking ourselves multilayered and mysterious makes the game of Bad Choice Monday Morning Quarterbacking fun. Example: In the Vanilla Ice Cream Paradigm, if you should find yourself giving a hand job to your ex in a Toyota Camry at two in the afternoon in a mall parking lot, simultaneously enjoying yourself and also squinting against the giant regret migraine you know will come in about twelve minutes, your behavior can be traced to exactly one cause: vanilla ice cream. But, if you follow Valery, the perfume of your indecency wafts up from possibly a) your inner dignity b) your inner hatred of capitalism, or even c) your inner innocent, unbending belief in true love. Now we're getting somewhere. Sorting all of this out could take days, months even, of solipsistic rumination. Magically, your weirdness mutates into a satisfying hobby instead of a source of shame. Is it possible that we've accidentally stumbled upon poetry's origin story?

Poems are perverse, willfully obscure little engines of narcissism—at best, irrelevant; at worst, ruinous to good citizenship. Or that's the allegation, anyway, and they've been trying to beat the rap since Plato. Is it possible that the reason poems are so fucked up, dangerous, or pointless is that poets themselves are so good on the inside? What a satisfying fiction.

Neatly, and in Order

It is a turbid, muddled, gothic sort of an affair, without a sweeping outline and with little pictorial nobility.
—William James, *A Pluralistic Universe*

As a kid I was a crier, a real Camille. I cried over baby animals. I cried when my parents fought. I cried if anyone was mean to me, or if I saw anybody be mean to anybody else. I could not watch *M*A*S*H* with the family because just the idea of war, even as a backdrop for punch lines, would have me in hysterics before the first commercial break. Nobody knew what to do with me. I wasn't interested in riding a bicycle or doing anything with a ball. I had no siblings, and other kids in the neighborhood understandably found me offputting. I did like books, though, and living in the world of pretend, so I read and read and read, and in reading I found relief and, more importantly, control over the constant overwhelming intensity of my feelings. Are other kids like this? I'm not sure. I mean obviously they don't all retreat from chaos into books (mine didn't) but does everyone find learning to negotiate their feelings so impossible? I like to imagine kinesthetic types, dancers and basketball players and runners, have it easier because their whole bodies work to express the excesses inside of them. I mostly just have words pummeling me inside my brain.

Turns out, reading was a pretty good strategy. I got the gold stars in school and eventually I even stopped crying. I think other kids still found me offputting, but I managed. Not until my thirties, when my therapist pointed out that I might "intellectualize my emotions" did I realize a potential downside to the chronic reading, which was that I habitually cushion myself from feeling with ideas, with argument. Theory as fear reducer and pain manager. In other words, I turned into a philosopher, and that's not a good thing. According to William James:

> Philosophers have always aimed at clearing up the litter with which the world is apparently filled. They have substituted economical and orderly conceptions for the first sensible tangle; and whether these were morally elevated or merely intellectually neat, they were at any rate always aesthetically pure and definite, and aimed at ascribing to the world something clean and intellectual.

Ouch. They don't call him the father of psychology for nothing. Even the phrase "intellectually neat" sort of thrills me, like a clean countertop. James describes the sterile pleasure of theorizing better than anyone. He describes me better than anyone, as if he knows how productive and capable I feel when my objective mind runs the show, but also how secretly lazy and rebellious. I, too, disdain the orderly conception even as I'm conceiving it, and resent my need for tidy causal packages. These "philosophers" he keeps ridiculing sound suspiciously familiar, in a "takes one to know one" kind of way.

After our most recent quarterly mass shooting for example, when everyone else was weeping and calling loved ones and going to vigils, I stayed up late, unable to sleep while I developed a point-by-point refutation of the idea of subcultural co-option because I feared it would reduce the groundswell of empathy necessary to enact gun reform. And I didn't do anything with it. I didn't shed one tear; I didn't write a congressman one check; I didn't even write down the thoughts in a journal. I just thought them until I could sleep. That cannot be healthy.

Of course any alcoholic can tell you that too much thinking is bad for you, but they don't tell you what to do instead. James, bless him, offers an alternative, but it's strong medicine. He says that compared with the pleasure of rationalizing, pragmatism, by which he means abandoning any hope that ideas can accurately correspond to a world out there, is a "turbid, muddled, gothic sort of affair without sweeping outline and little pictorial nobility," but one must live some time with a system to appreciate its merits. A master of gentle understatement, James nudges us to try out this new system of ditching systems, insinuating that we all might be better off with a little more present tense experiment and a little less rumination.

James himself did not arrive at this conclusion without plenty of staying up nights theorizing, inexplicably and inescapably driven to spend his time thinking about how he might limit the prison of his thinking. Chronically depressed, he wrote volumes on the fuel of his restless misery. But notice those delicious adjectives, *turbid*, *muddled*, *gothic*. Those don't come from analysis—they aren't even rhetorically sensible. They are, as Richard Rorty says, contingent meaning balanced somehow between private nonsense and public communication, between meaning and not meaning, the language of artists, because artists recognize the inertia of perfected speech and closed systems. Rorty says only poets can see the limits of the perfect and the closed, and the rest of us are "doomed to remain philosophers."

Recently underemployed for some weeks, I found myself getting enough sleep and exercise, cooking every meal, having plenty of sex, not reading much of anything, and generally just catering to the wants of my animal body. I had such plans for that time. I was going to submit my manuscript and write a new one and update my résumé and attend every meeting instead of dodging them like usual and possibly find a new career in marketing that would pay off my student debt and allow me to—what, exactly? Retire? Live on a houseboat and whittle? Devote myself entirely to internet shoe shopping? Die? I occasionally cast about in my notebooks for something of interest to say, and wow did I have fuck all. All my reason and reasons looked trivial. I re-read my poems and saw with some distress that every single one of them was an argument designed to explain away a wound or mystery. There's me, The Little Engine That Could, chuffing away in search of praise and answers and perfect understanding, even when I'm trying to make art.

Maybe I am doomed to be a philosopher. "A radical pragmatist" (or she who has successfully cut ties with theory), James says, "is a happy go lucky, anarchistic sort of creature...adrift in a tramp and vagrant world." Sounds like a Springer spaniel, but I can practically taste the longing in his voice. James was not that kind of pragmatist. He got shit done. Even though somehow, inadvertently, right there in the middle of his earnest striving, his language always runs away with him. One minute he lectures soberly on the nuances of Hegel and humanism, and the next he fills a page with lunacy, mocking what he calls "abstraction worship" with wild metaphors like "the bellyband of its universe must be tight" and "every drop of blood, every smallest item, appointed and provided, stamped and branded."

This doesn't sound to me like someone getting away from the intensity of feelings by theorizing. It sounds like someone falling face first into them while looking for something else. All that strange, iconoclastic whimsy—poetry disguised as philosophy, maybe. I guess what I am trying to say (besides William James is awesome, seriously, go read some William James) is that I may have just realized that I can meditate and eat gummy worms and roll around in the grass all I want but I still won't be that blissful pragmatist, not even a little bit zen. I still can't watch more than one episode of *Game of Thrones* at a time without being paralyzed by sorrow at the human condition. I'm just not a happy go lucky, anarchistic girl. I need those theory engines firing if I ever want to get to the art or find the feelings. And it's embarrassing and weird just like it was when I was ten, but there's no escaping it.

There is a Light That Never Goes Out

Death is no different whined at than withstood.
—Philip Larkin, "Aubade"

S, this gorgeous, freaky girl from Longview I used to know, so pretty that she always had pockets full of drugs from various dirtbags (and some genuinely nice guys) who wanted to fuck her and thought it might help, liked to share them with me. She and I would get high and drive around dark East Texas roads listening to The Smiths, singing our hearts out. She might be the only person ever to have heard me sing at full voice. She had the best music collection, and despite her funereal wardrobe, was radiantly sunny and full of joy. She loved drugs and dancing and music and makeup and intrigues and wild theorizing, and one night when I was twenty, she died on my living room floor from a heroin overdose.

I had gone to bed early. She was visiting. I didn't know about the heroin. Her other friends said that it wasn't a habit, and her naked body showed no injection sites, save the one. I remember looking at her torso, after the paramedics called it. I was in shock and it's all blurry now, but I knew immediately and clearly that the body meant something different than I thought it did.

I was a teenaged Goth Girl during peak AIDS crisis, reading pulp horror novels and writing poems about smoking. I thought about sex a lot, but death, I admit, stayed near fully repressed. I didn't indulge in fantasies of glamorous suicide like people I knew, or actual suicide, like some others. Church left its mark. Jesus died for sins still uncommitted in my case, so it was death, not sex that got shelved—"TBD." People died at regular intervals, as they do, but I think it didn't touch me. The taboo took.

When, ten years from his own death, Phillip Larkin wrote in "Aubade" that "Death is no different whined at than withstood," he was not only stoically alliterative, but also right. Nothing helps. Religion, he dismissed as "That vast moth-eaten musical brocade" and philosophy, "specious stuff." Maybe he felt poetry helped, since "Aubade" is the most unflinching poem about death I can think of. "Work has to be done," he says at the end, and that's the best he has to offer us. In his case, work was writing poems and being a librarian and confirmed bachelor. He must have been a smooth talker, because he still had lots of affairs despite a face like a boiled egg in glasses. No kids, though. After living through World War II in one of the most heavily bombed places in Europe, he probably saw enough suffering and death to regard it with equanimity. Terrible as it was, unlike sex, you could count on it.

Every Halloween, I set the table for the dead like Mom taught me, with pictures of beloved dogs, grandparents, and friends, along with candy, fruit, and booze, in case they come over. Maybe this is cool now, if the décor section of Freddie's is any indication, but when I was a kid, it was weird. Morbid. Even so, I taught my own kids how to do it, too. Do we do it to make friends with death? Is all that cheerful kitsch an attempt to create and connect in the face of our terrible temporary bodies? Or is it plain ole magical thinking? I grew up in a peaceful time, so in that way I'm still a child, believing life and afterlife continue forever, no end.

S's perfect corpse, no bruises, no nothing, looked empty, as if she had slipped out of herself for a smoke. At her services they said Jesus held her in his arms, that she smiled at us from heaven. She would have laughed if she'd heard that, but I found it pleasant. I felt blank—not exactly sad, but like a hole had been torn in the sky, and all you could do was stare and wonder. I got pregnant within the year, my baby born on S's birthday.

When sex showed up in earth's primal ocean, it helped our animal ancestors make new kinds of things and hurry evolution along. Death came with it, a natural consequence. Because our oldest relatives reproduced asexually by cloning, they were, in a sense, eternal. Death was the price paid for evolution towards individuation—towards people. Maybe the Goth Girl intuits this in her fishnet-encased bones. Making death sexy, or sex deathy, is her way of managing the twin pillars of reality, the consequences of which may be more real to her once she reaches reproducing age.

When I got pregnant, I developed phobias I hadn't had before—fear of flying, of cancer, of my own history poisoning me. The unthought thing started to seep out; the taboo unstuck. I have reproduced, and now I will die. And then, if I'm very lucky, my kids will reproduce, and then they will die. The sex part of my education is complete, the death part only beginning. I read "Aubade" like a ghost story, a way to give myself the willies. I know the second half of my life will contain more grief than the first, maybe so much that I will welcome life's end, but that feels too big to either whine at or withstand. Will I ever not like life? Honestly, I can't imagine.

Asylum Envy

An outbreak of severalness in the asylum of singularity
—Dean Young, "House of Geodes"

Literal meanings are packaged commodities for passive consumers. In poetry the reader is incorporated into the work, and all the Lord's people become prophets.
—Norman O. Brown, *Love's Body*

The other night I stormed out of a philosophy lecture in a state of high dudgeon. As I sat at the bar, alone and glowering, the nice gay waiter made the *Oh, honey* noise at me as if I'd been jilted, which infuriated me more. It wasn't his fault. I looked the part. I was alone on a Saturday night in a nice dress, wearing, I imagine, the bitch face to end all bitch faces. But somehow the lecture and the waiter and philosophy in general and men in general got all tangled up in my mind.

As if I have nothing better to do, I kept thinking, *than watch you jerk off.*

Who was I talking to? I'd come to the lecture of my own free will, not like getting dragged to church or anything. And philosophers are just regular folks trying to puzzle things out like the rest of us, right? So what if he went long, re-explaining the point he could have made twice as elegantly in half the time? Maybe the rest of the audience wanted that overdetermined demonstration of onanistic pyrotechnics. Maybe they liked having the blanks filled in for them.

Well I don't want my blanks filled against my will.

Jesus Christ. Clearly, I'd stumbled into some land mine of buried misandry that (hopefully) only exists with regard to philosophy. I wish this feeling didn't have to do with gender, but I'm afraid it must, otherwise why all the genital metaphors? Why the poor waiter? Why did it feel like church, or, like a friend says, "flipping the bird at a closed door?"

Norman O. Brown says in *Love's Body* that in poetry the reader is incorporated into the gaps between meanings, so that "all the Lord's people become prophets." Maybe it's my Protestant background, or maybe just megalomania, but I want to be a prophet. I want my language to do everything that Freud's and Hegel's does, but more elegantly, and in one hundred words or less. I want to leave gaps in the meaning as profound as entire books, and I want everyone to cheer. I also want, at sixty, to be smug, beaming, forty pounds overweight from all the expensive dinners I eat in out-of-town restaurants, and in general so replete with cultural capital that people wait in line to hear me blather.

Not really.

(But sort of.)

It's funny to me that the only time I ever experience what by now I'm sure every armchair psychoanalyst reading this has accurately diagnosed as penis envy is in the world of books and ideas. Same place it came from. Freud learned a few things talking to all those smart neurotic women about what happens when intelligence coupled with a cast iron ego goes to waste. And I often wonder what would have happened to me as a writer and a person if I ever felt like I had infinite space and time to communicate whatever zany idea came into my little head. Would I have been a philosopher instead of a poet? Richard Rorty says only poets are free from the literal and the rest of us are "doomed to remain philosophers." This comforts me, but I won't lie; my desire to generate some new theory, some new grand design, runs deep.

Still, my favorite poetic form is the sonnet. Sixteen lines to make an argument. That's all you get to convince the reader or the beloved or yourself of your grand design. Strictly formal, and yet the best ones sound like they just fell out bed, tousled and perfect. They're tiny things of great beauty, hard to make but cheap to buy. Like doll house furniture.

Behavior is a Pile of Clothes

I meant behavior
is a pile of clothes

I might or might not wear.
—Rae Armantrout, "Life's Work"

There's a neighbor girl down the street, not a girl I guess, maybe thirty, who talks to me at our neighborhood bar, about my clothes, my shoes, my perfume. She sees me walking to work in the morning and remembers until next we meet. It's a tenuous basis for a friendship, but I do like the attention, and the way she seems to attribute to me a kind of person that I am not. I especially enjoy it from her because she's lovely, plush and painted and glossy, but in a young way. It might be that she makes me feel old, because if I extended that kind of effort in my toilette, I would look hard. And yes, these are the things I think about, and was thinking about, even during the election season.

A woman was almost president, and she was decidedly unbeautiful, hideously not young, dressed in DC frumpery and groomed like a Kansas City Mother of the Bride.

Behavior is a pile of clothes. Those clothes, and that they were not quite right, may have cost her the race to someone so repellent on every level that even she had a shot against a man in an expensive suit. The earnestness of her dress was no small matter. She could not look expensive without class critique. She could not look butch. She could not look as if she cared, but it was absolutely forbidden for her to look as if she didn't. The higher the stakes, the more of a sartorial knife's edge she had to walk, and this rule is ironclad for all of us gals.

I remember how I loved Martha Stewart for wearing a mink scarf to her insider trading trial. She went, I'd wager, to jail over that fur. But not all of us can afford to flout the rules. Some of us need to eat.

For Halloween this year, a friend sewed her own blow-up doll costume out of vinyl and a flesh colored bodysuit. She has a genius for fabrics, and creative expression of every variety. When I showed her a photograph of herself in this creepy, perfect, elaborate, remarkable ensemble, she said: "Oh, god, I look fat in that picture." Behavior is a pile of clothes, and behavior becomes habit becomes character.

I never leave the house without thinking about it. I might or might not wear any number of numbers, carefully chosen with my own character in mind. I dress myself to play myself as an unselfconscious and artful type. Jersey for ease of movement, heels for poise, structure for discipline, and print for whimsy. Each of these choices influence my behavior in subtle and obvious ways, but more importantly, they influence others' behavior toward me. Too much cleavage and I'll be underestimated (though this can be useful). Too much black and I'll intimidate (this too). Too lush a fabric says "I don't need this job," but too cheap says I don't deserve it. I might be shallow, but I might not. I am one of those who has to eat, and if a larger portion of my budget goes to my wardrobe than you think is wise, think of Lily Bart, Meg March, Emma Bovary. "We are expected to be pretty and well-dressed till we drop," remarks Lily in *House of Mirth*. And Lily does drop, at her own hand, at least partially due to wardrobe mismanagement. Had she only been pretty and well-dressed enough without accessorizing too much, would there have been a happy ending? Would she have won the husband? The job? The election?

This is a sensitive subject for me, as I recently lost my job to a man with drastically less experience and skill than myself. This man also liked to talk about my clothes, and so did our boss. He liked to call me "the pretty lady" in front of clients. He also wore shorts to the office, I guess to demonstrate how little these trappings of propriety affected him. It didn't occur to me to mind it too much. I never complained. I mean, in the hierarchy of inappropriate comments I've heard about my appearance, this seemed like small potatoes. I'm content to be thought pretty as long as I'm also thought capable.

I might or might not dress in a way as to incur that kind of attention, but I did. I do. And in retrospect it burns, because all of my behavior was reduced to a pile of clothes, despite whatever else I had to offer. I wonder if I had been slovenly, or plain, would I have been evaluated fairly? Or would that too have been worthy of remark—just not to my face.

Meditations on Aesthetics

This is not an age of beauty...
My heart believes it is a muscle
of love, so how do I tell it it is a muscle of blood?
—Emilia Phillips, "Age of Beauty"

I wish it were an age of beauty. Just because there's plenty of it around doesn't mean we appreciate or understand it. I feel ashamed of how much beauty matters to me, how much time I spend admiring my husband's thick hair and strong back. I know I am supposed to love him for his character, and I do, of course, but I also love him for the elegance of his hands and his sharp jaw. Beauty is not democracy. It is a tyranny, and a master I constantly struggle not to resent, because I love fine perfume and paintings of fat naked women and silver art deco mirrors and elegant language and the silk scarf on that girl on the train this morning, its blue brightening her yellow hair. I don't know how to make peace with beauty. Our current culture's major lines of rhetoric are, at best, moralizing lies, and at worst, insane.

ONE: *Beauty is Objective*: The draconian model of beauty as either rare and expensive or exhausting and time consuming. A walk outside refutes this. Smiling two-year-olds, fat purple pigeons, flowers, sunsets everywhere—all common as dirt.

TWO: *Beauty is Subjective*: The patronizing fairy tale that we are all equally beautiful "in our own way." Or "on the inside." This is cold comfort to anyone who has ever felt the sting of romantic rejection, or watched an even-featured moron steal every scrap of attention in a room.

THREE: *Beauty is Irrelevant*: Come the revolution, such lookist preoccupations will dissolve into an egalitarian ether. For better or worse, as long as there's desire, people will still be preoccupied. They will just pretend harder that they love you for your mind.

FOUR: *Beauty is a Mating Strategy*: In order to secure resources for your offspring you must fool mates into seeing your assets as more symmetrical and youthful than the competition's assets, and you must do it now, for the sands of time run quickly and the world mints new twenty-two-year-olds every day. Maybe, but I like to look at pretty girls, too. Though they provide me no reproductive opportunities, they still decorate the world.

FIVE: *Beauty is Evil*: Take off that lipstick, you look like a whore. If I had a dime for every time I heard some Gen X-er decry Instagram girls, selfies, or the endless cash women spend on shallow garbage like Tom Ford eyeliner, I could take a year off, get some rest and a chin lift. Maybe then I wouldn't feel quite so judgmental about young girls using new technology to do the same old things.

IF IT TRULY were an age of beauty, we would have better theories. Or at least more respect for the terrible power of it, how it demands our attention and shapes our experience from the moment we open our eyes.

I always ask my female friends if their mother was beautiful, because it tells you so much about how they see themselves. I had a beautiful mother who hated her looks, though thankfully she kept that second part quiet most of the time. I prayed to be beautiful like her. I was not. I hoped I might overcome the shallow longing for it, be interesting looking instead. I hoped the rewards of noble transcendence might outweigh the rewards of adoration and glances and love and the pleasure of seeing my own face in the mirror. It did not. I eventually grew more beautiful, of course, as young girls do, but I couldn't see any of it, and it did me no good.

And still, the barometer of my self-loathing day to day, whatever its cause—a fight with a friend, a failure at work—is directly perceivable to me in the mirror. On my best days, I look fine, lovely even. The worst, I'm repulsive—a lumpen, quivering mass of chins. Knowing both are hallucinations made of brain chemicals and social comparison hardly helps, though sometimes the effect is so sudden it makes me laugh out loud. The first three months after I quit smoking, I was monstrous, every single day. I had not heard tell of this side effect, but it nearly broke me, lung cancer be damned. Thankfully, a casual female acquaintance who quit the year before mentioned that it happened to her, too, and that it did go away eventually. Bless her.

I think this wrestling with beauty is especially difficult for people who concern themselves with aesthetics. I carry a medium sized burlap bindle of commonplace anxiety about my looks, but a train car of existential anxiety about my tastes. I make irrationally powerful and immediate decisions about what I like and don't like to look at. This has more far-reaching effects than you might think, and I find it an ugly feature of my character. I'd rather not be the sort of person capable of looking at a work of art or a human being and thinking, *Ugh*. But I am that sort of person. It's awfully hard to convince yourself that beauty doesn't equal love when you know in your own dark heart that you love what it beautiful, and you can't help it.

A Jar

All we can say in the face of our insane tribulations were that they were an act of love.
—Mary Ruefle, "On Sentimentality"

My blood pressure shot so high the last time the doctor checked it, they wanted me to go to the hospital. Are you short of breath? he said, Do your feet feel numb? No, actually, I feel fine. I always feel fine. He sent me home with a refill of my lapsed prescription and a stern warning. To do what? Oh yes, to buy a blood pressure cuff. He did not say I should quit talking to my family, who, like everybody's family, are a nexus of insane tribulations. They've been rough on me lately, but they love me they love me they love me, and I don't feel that, either. My body is a sealed jar of three generations worth of undigested, burbling discord and apparently I'd rather have an aneurysm than take the lid off.

At least I'm not the only one. High blood pressure runs in my family, along with alcoholism and anxiety disorders. Scattered across the continent but still connected by social media and genetics, my cousins and I all look remarkably alike, with the same German chin and the same fat, bald babies. My cousin D and I were born a week apart to sisters. Her mother died young and she helps me take care of mine. She just texted me yesterday:

> Got the BP down from STROKE to prehypertension—STOKED

Me and this girl used to go to the roller rink together. We used to play mermaids in a plastic swimming pool. In my memory, our entire childhood consisted of one long game of pretend, in which we practiced every kind of grown up feeling we could imagine: lust, envy, jealousy, rage, triumph, humiliation, romance, sorrow—the works. The stories that went along with the feelings were immaterial, just hooks to hang the passion on, and we loved every minute of it. Of course there were some adult feelings we couldn't imagine. The still ones: ambivalence, regret, resignation, contentment, because those tend to be invisible, and also they aren't as much fun.

Now she's a professional disciplinarian. This means she spanks people who pay her well, with every implement one could imagine, and her clients can imagine quite a lot. Just like when we were kids, the plot points don't seem as important as the feelings. I just watched a clip of hers for this column where she paddles a sweet old man with twelve different kinds of hair brush. It may sound like a droll domestic cartoon, but make no mistake, a wooden hairbrush, forcefully applied, can do some real damage. He's obviously old and vulnerable, though you can't see his face, and she's impermeable as a sphinx. She's taking care of him. She's helping him unscrew the lid on his jar.

She looks beautiful, and so, so poised. The lady-est of ladies, and while I watch I can see the power in her witnessing other peoples' insane tribulations, to take them in and hold still, to transform them with compassion, like water to wine. But I also see the psychic residue it leaves on her. He weeps and screams and rails against the injustice of it all, and it's obvious that this release is better, for him, than sex, or therapy, or whatever else people use to expunge the bile inside of them. And though I know the method wouldn't work for me, I feel envy.

She says, "It's a good job for people with our temperament."

My dear friend C just told me today her mother is dying of cancer. Dying dying. Six months, maybe a year. C's another professional caretaker, a nurse practitioner. Her lid's on tight, too—birds of a feather. She grew up with D and me. We talk on the phone and she's a soldier, taking care of everything, praying, working to pay for it all, and yet she's still troubled in her heart because her mother makes her insane and she can't connect with her grief. She's what they'd call a "tough cookie."

Imagine you are one.

You're straight and stone-sturdy while everything else goes apart around you. You're crazier than everyone else from always pretending to be sane. It fills you with shame. Because you want to feel as big as you used to, to give your beloveds the gift of your suffering, to experience the empathy that cleanses petty resentments and gives you the delicious pleasure of intimacy. But the act of love, the verb of it, requires that you don't feel too much, therefore making space for other people to feel more intensely—to be like a child in your arms and know you can take it.

Love, Revised

To see you again, isn't love revision?
—Brenda Shaughnessy, "One Love Story, Eight Takes"

Two years ago my daughter told me she wanted to try out living as a boy for a while. We were talking in our tiny bathroom, me in the tub and her sitting on the toilet—ever since she was little, or rather just past big enough to take a bath with me, she would come and find me in the tub, where it was warm and private, to tell me important things. She winced through the confession as if she expected a balloon to pop, and the relief in her face and body and trembling voice shimmered in the air like gasoline. I cannot imagine how hard that must have been. She was what, seventeen, eighteen?, and on her way out of our house, our bathroom, our everyday intimacies of dinners and chores. I felt a space open up next to me as vast as, well...space. I hope I was kind, and my face did not betray the vertigo I felt. I think I was glib. Not mean or hysterical, I said, "Maybe you should cut your hair short and get a girlfriend first."

Of course I'd had short hair, and girlfriends, and gender confusion of various stripes—mostly about what kind of girl I would be—but I always knew I wanted to "become," like Simone says, a woman. I wanted the clothes, the freedom of expression, the license to move with grace and to gesture, and to make babies like some kind of superhero, and no matter how routinely I saw its deficits, both material and spiritual, no matter (or perhaps because of) the violence and the compression, I still secretly believed adult women were supreme beings. How then to handle this decampment from grace by my very own flesh?

Intellectually, politically, socially, and out loud I took the news in stride. I would will myself into the words I said and knew—though somewhere far away—to be true. Except that every time I talked about it, my eyes would fill with tears. I couldn't feel it, quite. It felt like a nervous tic. What was I sad about? My gorgeous, funny, talented, kind, and exceptionally self-aware child was still around, still all those things. Her body belonged to her, something I told her as many times as I could remember to. I was only the guardian. Her body was hers to be his if he so desired, and this became my mantra in the coming weeks. *Not my body not my choice not my body not my choice*, over and over until the words began slowly to gain ground.

In the poem "One Love Story, Eight Takes," Brenda Shaughnessy asks, "Isn't love revision?" I like that she asks instead of tells and the question is not rhetorical. It's a real, live question, a squirmy not-knowing. Is love revision? If it is, then I must learn to love my son as effortlessly and automatically as I loved my daughter. Loved. Is not love revision? When we lose love, through death or other cosmic rent in the universe, notlove becomes the space we must accommodate. I can't love my daughter anymore, because she no longer exists except in memory. Now, two years after we first spoke of it, even the name I gave her is gone.

But the love remains. The love does not get revised. It envelops me and my newborn son and settles into the hole my daughter left like a missing tooth. He is very much like her; I am tempted to say exactly like her, but that is only wishful thinking. He is exactly like himself, except without the terrible burden of pretense. Somewhere, in the process of becoming what I dreamed for him, a new vision I could not have imagined took hold. I could not imagine it because he is not me, and this, the most simple and tragic lesson of motherhood, rewrites everything I thought I already knew. His body belongs to him now.

Ruin

O didn't you know I'd been ruined? said she.
—Thomas Hardy, "The Ruined Maid"

Did you know that a wedding gown weighs roughly the same as a fat toddler? Did you know that you need help to put the thing on, and that bits of beadwork will snag against your underwear, or worse, your underwear or nails might snag the satin? I didn't know any of this. I knew wedding gowns were outrageously expensive, and unwearable except for the once, and that I should experience some kind of frisson of beauty and meaning when I found the "right" one. Instead I skulked from one store to another, alone, too embarrassed to even drag a girlfriend along. I had no idea what I wanted, except that it wouldn't be white, wouldn't have lace, no veil, no strapless, no sweetheart neck, nothing bridal. I finally gave up when, forlorn in the last store I tried, I asked the sweet young thing in the showroom if they had anything in cotton. She smiled and leaned in to me. "I think you're in the wrong place," she whispered.

I've always had a terror of weddings. Where I come from, people marry for sport, penance, or profit. Most adult women I knew growing up had been married at least twice. Divorce, infidelity, operatic fights and heartfelt reconciliations and recommitments in church—all common as dirt. I remember my mother and her friends laughing over a particularly expensive and saccharine invitation, heavy emphasis on words like "forever" and "before God." This was, if I remember correctly, the woman's fourth wedding. My wedding phobia is not new. I know that I have it, and why, and I even think it wise and just, but still I am getting married and I'm happy about it, happy about my sweetheart joining teams with me, despite the dress paralysis.

At the risk of sounding immodest, I usually excel at all things femme-y—the concrete things, like eyeliner and pot roast, and the not-so-concrete things: compliments, mom-voice, social maintenance. I've been good at being a girl for a long, long time, and more importantly, I've always enjoyed it. It's just that despite my extensive Barbie collection, I only had one Ken, if you know what I mean. I never dreamed about my wedding cake or wedding dress. When a friend says, "Only you know your vision for this day," I wince. I never had a vision. I wanted to be a mermaid, or possibly Harriet the Spy.

Later, when I started getting crushes, having sex, falling in love, I had a different vision. I didn't escape romanticism, but I wanted to be an adventuress. I wanted lovers and a walk-up in a big city. I wanted to be an artist with a complicated and stormy series of passionate entanglements. I wanted out of the trap of what Angela Carter calls "feminine impotence—a mode of experience that transcends gender." I may not have known what to call it, but I did know that in the real world, girlish vulnerability invites harm. Purity is danger. To be a feminine woman and also have agency and a reasonable expectation of safety has always been hard to pull off. Tomboys and butches manage by eschewing femininity altogether (see Harriet the Spy). Or if you want to keep your lipstick and black underwear, you can always choose the path of economic free agency. Signaling to the world at large that you are no longer pure by adopting the persona of an "experienced" woman (or, you know, a whore) provides at least some armor against would be despoilers.

So this wedding thing—the nameless anxiety and dread I feel when friends suggest I take a quick look at Pinterest—maybe it's nothing more than a good old fashioned Madonna-whore complex. I don't know why it never occurred to me I might have one, considering how many times I heard Mom say, "Never, ever rely on a man to support you." The whore, Carter says, despite her eviction from polite society, "stands for the old fashioned virtues of self reliance" and her femininity is "part of her arsenal of self interest." And though art and literature may be full of fearsome tales of punishment for whores, we sense in them something aspirational. Like gay men, they represent freedom from reproduction and matrimony, a heaven of disposable income and sexual novelty.

Thomas Hardy, the Lars Von Trier of the *fin de siècle*, who made a career of devising horrific punishments for tender virgins like poor Tess of the d'Urbervilles, does give us at least one whore heroine who makes it out alive—'Melia, from the poem "The Ruined Maid":

"O 'Melia my dear, this does everything crown!
Who could have supposed I should meet you in Town?
And whence such fair garments such prosperi-ty?" —
"O didn't you know I'd been ruined?" said she.

"Ruin," Hardy suggests, despite the bad PR, actually offers an alternate Happily Ever After. Like marriage, ruination is eternal. In its idealized state, you get good clothes, world travel, a whopping self care budget, time to sleep till noon and study French, and you don't have to sleep with the same guy your whole life, either. Of course, in its real world state, you get a range of outcomes—just like marriage. Hardy knows that to move from one class to another, quickly and without too much indignity, seems to require one or the other strategy. For men, the Madonna-whore complex means negotiating the false distinction between nurture and eroticism, but for women the choice is economic. Hardy never loses sight of this, whether in comic or tragic mode. 'Melia, in her fine dress and elevated speech, unmasks the hypocrisy of those Victorian virtues without dying for it, and I can't help but cheer every time I read her.

So it's no wonder that the white dress feels like a flag of surrender. I'm caught up in a pretend game of Love versus Freedom. That these psychic underpinnings remain hidden until I have to throw an expensive party show me just how lucky I am, and also what a hypocrite. All my fretting over symbols and how they operate in my self concept? Entertainment purposes only. By sheer random chance, born the right time, right place, right color, I can have anything I want. My choices about who and when and how I fuck, whether or not I get married in white or have lovers until I'm eighty, impact my safety and quality of life not at all, and if that makes me finally unfeminine, no longer "impotent" in Carter's formulation, then so be it. I'll take the virility.

A Public Apology

Man must be pleased; but him to please
Is woman's pleasure; down the gulf
Of his condoled necessities
She casts her best, she flings herself...
—Coventry Patmore, "Angel in the House"

Virginia Woolf said that it was the woman writer's job to kill the "Angel in the House," Coventry Patmore's shimmering chimera of fantastical femininity. The poem is a fluff piece fit for middlebrow tastes at best, but for whatever reason, the idea caught our imagination and stuck around for decades, alternately torturing and pacifying us with treacle. A feature of the English novel since forever, the morally superior woman is, to be honest, kind of comforting, maybe because we still like to fancy ourselves capable of transforming beasts into princes without doing much besides silently radiating virginity. We figured by now these Clarissas and Pamelas had peaceably rotted into fairy dust, along with their dark, sexually voracious, hysterical sisters drawing otherwise good men to psychological ruin and bankruptcy. I hoped so too, or hoped they had at least slunk back into their Regency novels, along with the wolves and roués (and reformed wolves and roués) to throw themselves on chaises and die of consumption or get married at long last, forever and ever amen.

But lately, as I watch the internet parade of public apologies for sexual misconduct—these gleefully tawdry stories of girls brought low by the lusts of powerful men—I'm not so sure. The motivations behind these stories seem suspect, although I doubt I'm supposed to say what I actually think—which is that a late and very public revelation is only a good strategy if the circles you run in are content worthy. For the rest of us, time is up about two seconds after your boundaries are violated.

And look, I know that's not always possible, but plenty of times it is, and where I grew up, those deer-in-the-headlights girls, those hesitating, eager to please types, their lives were ruined in ways that no one reading *Jezebel* wants to hear about. No triumph, no survivor stories, just crushed into dirt, usually more than once, and their families with them. A working class nobody who can't protect herself with meanness or resourcefulness in the moment also can't wait for HR or a think piece to save her. She may only have herself, and she can't afford to see her institutions as *in loco parentis*.

Stuck sorting out the (admittedly more urgent) patriarchal problem of male sexual entitlement, we may have overlooked that other patriarchal problem, the myth of the good girl, the angel, the innocent victim traumatized by our bloody sexual revolution, unable to survive this cruel world without chaperones. I think we might still in our secret hearts believe in her. She's Anastasia Steele and Bella Swan, and we can't get enough of getting rescued, at least in our imaginations. She makes us doubt our own ability to navigate our lives, to trust that we can manage the gropers, the cat calls, the white house, and much, heartbreakingly much, worse. Instead of strength she has virtue, and virtue doesn't keep you safe.

Most adult women I know in real life are pretty tough, and capable of real mayhem, especially when they are righteously pissed, generally, about the state of things. When you (I mean me) feel powerless publicly, you might be more likely to exploit what power you do have privately. And despite our physical and systemic vulnerabilities, women do have sexual power, though we often won't admit it. We are the ones biology gifted with the job of mate selection, and none of us are doing any public apologizing, even though we probably owe a few. Like Sade says of his wrathful anti-heroines, "one is never so dangerous when one has no shame, than when one has grown too old to blush." More of us should be dangerous.

Admitting you can do damage may be the first step toward empowerment. So here I go—in the interests of sexual equality and also to poke a sharp stick at the contemporary angel:

I Hereby Issue a Public Apology for My Lack of Sexual Integrity

I'm sorry for the derisive nicknames I gave to insensitive or awkward lovers, to make my friends laugh, which then followed said lovers forever.

I'm sorry for revealing embarrassing details of a man's anatomy or sexual habits if he hurt my feelings or my pride.

I'm sorry for the times I purposefully emasculated someone because I felt cornered.

I'm sorry for that drink in the face.

I'm sorry for the times I seduced someone I didn't care about, for ego validation or vengeance against another.

I'm sorry for the times I flirted casually with another's sweetheart, or when I myself was taken, therefore creating distrust or chaos, just because I was bored.

I am sorry for the times I broke someone's heart because I lied to myself about my feelings, or because I was too lazy to do the right, difficult thing.

I am sorry for the times I was inconsiderate because I bought the convenient lie that men don't have feelings, or that they would rather get laid than treated like a person.

I am sorry for the times I was cruel because I was mad—at my dad, at the world, at the unfairness of it all—and took it out on some poor dude who was just trying figure it out like I was.

Okay, that was rough. But the other night I dreamed a recurring dream: that I murdered someone years ago, and the body is about to be discovered under the basement dirt. I wake up sick with guilt and shame, relieved to see my sweetheart safe asleep beside me. Maybe the reformed wolf is me, and he's the angel in the house, "casting his best" and all that, though I'm sure he has his own long list of amends to make. Nobody is really pure, not even children.

Praying to Nina Simone

You have to improve your portrait of God
To make it plain.
—John Ashbery, "We Hesitate"

Because I'm an old fashioned agnostic, my friends and relations, atheist and Jesus-y alike, all believe I'm right thinking, and that I secretly side with them but am just too humanist to say so. True, I have been called a fence sitter, but mostly by myself. Raised by Baptists and sci-fi reading hippies, I developed my relationship with God early. On the one hand he was a handsome blond, and on the other he was more like the Force, a non-material mandala of goodies that sort of floated in the empty spaces and made the flowers grow. At night, after my mother kissed me and told me to say my prayers, I would try to imagine what, exactly, I was praying to until I fell asleep. Was God a boy or a girl? Did It have a face? Was It more like a horse or dirt or a ghost? I rarely got around to asking for anything, but the practice put a permanently spiritual kink in my imagination.

I still pray like that, though I don't call it praying unless I'm reassuring a relative that I will worry about a situation I have no control over, in God's honor. More often, I will ask those same relatives to worry/pray for me. I tell them I'm pretty sure they've got a better relationship with the Almighty than I have. They laugh shyly; everybody likes to be told they're right with Jesus. I'm not sure what good I think I'm doing asking people to pray for me, but it soothes me to know that someone is holding me in their mind right next to their highest value. It's a gift I wish I could give them, but the closest I ever get is in some mental cul-de-sac with karma and Darwin.

I asked my childhood friend Cynthia what she thought God looked like, and her first answer was that It was like a fiery luminescence with a gentle face you could see from every angle, which sounded a bit like my old floating mandala, an idea hovering tenously between being and abstraction. Then, she sent me this passage from Revelation 1:14:

> The hair on his head was white like wool, as white as snow, and his eyes were like blazing fire. His feet were like bronze glowing in a furnace, and his voice was like the sound of rushing waters. In his right hand he held seven stars, and coming out of his mouth was a sharp, double-edged sword. His face was like the sun shining in all its brilliance.

Yikes. Classic white guy in the sky. I mean, I get it—I get how one might need to have a picture in your head of a real person, no matter how glowing or large, that you could play chess with or lay your head down in his lap, but clearly that's not the right picture for me. My mother refers to God as Goddess, likes to pray to a fat woman with abundant hair. Whenever I try to imagine God as a person, all I can come up with is a bald intersex baby with tragic eyes and a voice like Nina Simone. And that's just silly.

But perhaps this is why I can never completely be free of the desire to see God in my mind (even though I am more content with a mystery than I ever would be with an answer): I've learned to associate my own lack of faith with a failure of the imagination. Because the first things I tried hard to imagine carved a hole in me that only moral contemplation ever fills. Because what Ashbery is directing us to do is to make something real out of our own highest value. Art may just be us picturing God, over and over again.

What a Monster

Huffy Henry hid the day,
unappeasable Henry sulked.
—John Berryman, "Dream Song 1"

My baby boy Hank, home for the summer, points out that I have not memorialized him in print yet, despite my oversharing about everyone else I know. And he is correct, partially because I assumed that at nineteen maybe he would rather die than have his mother talk publicly about how much she adores him. Hi, Henry. Unlike his elder sibling, the child does not radiate sunny extroversion. He's too busy plotting how to retire by thirty-five. Driven, competitive since birth, brilliant, private, neurotic, and funny, all his childhood stories, playing chess or bobbing for apples, sound like Icarus, every moment another opportunity for glory or destitution. I used to recite John Berryman, my other favorite megalomaniac, to him when he came home in a mood:

Huffy Henry hid the day
unappeasable, Henry sulked.

He hated it, but still he developed a good ear over the years. I like to think it came partially from all the reciting, then the mocking of the reciting, finished off by Kendrick Lamar, of whom we could say the same as critic Christopher Benfey said of Berryman: "his real and abiding muse was American spoken English." I've heard enough of Kendrick Lamar to carry on a passably cogent conversation about the relative merits of *Damn* versus to *To Pimp a Butterfly*, so we're a club of mutual influence. I give him books for Christmas he doesn't read, and he makes me look at sneakers online while we play the world's longest game of "would you rather." Would you rather have a million dollars in pennies or 500,000 in Bitcoin? Would you rather pretend to be racist at work for a week, or in a bar on a Saturday night for three hours? Would you punch Grandma in the face for ten thousand dollars? Who do you love the most?

All this we share, the shoe love, the language love, the dark imagination; it is very odd to see my own personality quirks assert themselves in a young man. He says things I never would dare to say out loud, even at my most entitled—like that he's the smartest person he knows, that he will make records and movies or maybe invent something—and I feel envy and amazement. If I had been a boy, would I have liked the craven, power-mad part of myself a little better? Would I have taken over the world? Did I give it to him like my own shadow, this ferocious need to win, to be a baller, to be famous, to buy his mama a house one day? Or is it just the regular old hubris of a young man? He says, "Everybody who makes it in this world acts like they can, and even that doesn't work for everyone." Maybe I should take his advice.

Berryman said of his mother, "All my vanity is based on her uncritical passionate admiration." And I think, Yes. I did that. Not only out of a "parent of a millennial" impulse to give everyone a trophy, but because I really do admire him, and because I can't wait to find out what becomes of a creative person a little like me, except without any shame about ambition. I am old enough to have heard many times that nobody likes a girl with a smart mouth. Not to talk too much. That I could always teach. And like the good little listener I grew into, I feel inadequate every single day I breathe, haunted by a pervasive fear of unearned arrogance, of too muchness.

So it's possible I overcorrected with my boys. Maybe I made them unappeasable, filling their heads with all the things they might want if they were brave. You never mean to give your kids the dreams you didn't finish, but they seem to inherit them anyway. John Berryman's mother created a monster, they say, but what a monster. The unchained aliveness of his work, the ferocious celebration of ego, the nerve—if she's at fault, the world should thank her.

Age of Contemplation

a pause   a little emptiness
each year harder to live within
each year harder to live without
—Craig Arnold, "Meditation on a Grapefruit"

I have been meditating for over a year now, spurred as I was by soul unraveling anxiety, both from regular and irregular circumstances. For one, I was born into chaos, which marked me forever as the kind of person who can hear a change in tone or a change in the weather like a dog whistle. If there's trouble coming, I usually know, even if mostly I can't do anything about it. Two, I raised kids alone, at times unbearably so, and somewhere along the trajectory of those years, my mind and my body agreed we would just have to fall apart later. I doubt my fragile state during those years was a mystery to anyone but myself. I drank too much, ate fistfuls of candy, smoked, worked very hard, kept a reasonably clean house, and a full fridge. No car, two jobs, no spouse. Ordinary American working class accomplishments, but difficult enough for me that it frayed my cords until they shot sparks. It's a miracle I never caught fire.

Then I got married, the kids grew up and moved out, and in the ensuing peace and quiet I finally heard my racing heart, loud, and my racing thoughts, ticking off item after item on the master list of my failures. I didn't write enough. I drank too much coffee. I was a real bitch yesterday, or the day before, or six years ago. Waves of panic I must have been using to keep the machine running for years suddenly had nowhere to go. My mind was like a fist, clenched for so long that when I released it, the sensation nearly knocked me over.

In short, I did not start meditating because I wanted spiritual fulfillment, I started meditating because I thought I might lose my marbles. Craig Arnold describes meditation in his poem "Meditations on a Grapefruit" as "a little pause   a little emptiness/harder each year to live within/ harder each year to live without." I did not know I needed a pause to live in until I started carving one with a spoon, only to watch the depression fill with nonsense, nearly as fast as I could empty it. Maybe that's the image Arnold saw too, rising in the triangular pools in the fruit, his own puzzled face.

Life, says the Buddha, is suffering, but I never really believed that. I smile at strangers. I like my house and my people, and I live in a world of plenty. It would be obnoxious, not to mention ungrateful, to see my life as misery. The suffering glides quietly under the surface. Old stuff, new stuff, money. But when a crack appears, the whole world gets soaked with it, and as the years accrue, it gets harder for me to let the breeze in and dry out the damp.

I'm not great at it; it usually feels like trying not to eavesdrop on the world's most boring conversation. I project all my self-loathing onto poor Elizabeth Gilbert.

(Sorry, Elizabeth. I'm sure you're a perfectly nice person.) I remember to call my mother, I get fantastic ideas about what to write that I know I won't remember unless I stop immediately and get a pen. I feel goofy admitting this, but I'm often plagued by embarrassment, as if I'm John Wayne and afraid the other cowboys will call me a fairy. I feel like a fraud and a first class magical thinker, six months away from a weekend aura-reading workshop. How could sitting with my eyes closed do anything? The answer is I don't know. Placebo effect?

We know little about the ancient Vedic people who first described the empty mind, the atman, or the witnessing soul, because they didn't build much, and what they did build they set on fire for ritual purposes. I love ritual purposes; they make me feel stitched tight to my spot here in space-time. Maybe meditation is just ritualized lying about, and I'm excellent at that. If I sound glib, I don't mean to. It's tricky to talk about any of this for fear of awkwardly stomping on someone else's sacred principles with my size ten American feet, but I will say that those Vedic people left us some durable psychic technology, a gift I could never have guessed I would need as much as I do now.

The Devil Says Maybe I Like It

For all men, certainly all imaginative men, must be for ever casting forth enchantments.
—W.B. Yeats, *Ideas of Good and Evil*

Would it surprise anyone to learn I had a tarot deck or five? Or that I pray/meditate/sage the house when I have unwanted visitors? Despite my (thin) materialist façade and Woo Contempt (obvious projection), I have practiced witchcraft of one form or another for my entire adult life, mostly out of habit and home training. Keep track of the phases of the moon; throw salt; drink dandelion tea on your period; write your bad habits and burn them, drown them, tie them with string. OCD begins in a mind gripped with obsession, one of those minds whose contents seem more real than the external world. The compulsions ritualize action to ameliorate the paralysis of the obsession. They grease a stuck wheel and make forward motion possible.

I DRAW the Empress card. The first step to enlightenment is sensuality. She's a still, big girl in an oversized nightgown. She symbolizes devious, prodigious nature. Exasperating. I am a big, still girl—I don't need a reminder. I need a Knight of Wands or something else dynamic, The Chariot. I call Mom. Unfortunately, she always says I'll be fine, fantastic even. Mother love drowns bad news. But some days I am not fine and I need practical guidance. I was not reared by utilitarians, and what skills I have in that arena came late and were hard won. I understand mystical symbols, though, and know how to put them to use—relatively practical, all things considered.

MY PERSONAL card is Temperance. I don't wait to draw it; I keep one in my bag for courage. Reason unspecified, I've just always liked it—it makes me think of a duck paddling madly under the smooth surface of a pond. On the inside, I am intemperate—a bucket of cross-purposes, a real maniac. I can't make a decision. Too deregulated. I'm petty and horny and vain. Outside, I aim for equipoise.

The cards—the concrete acting out of desired outcomes (ritual)—suit me, maybe because there's nothing out there insisting I believe without method. Also, it works. Not in a "closet full of furs" way, but by changing your consciousness just enough to feel less powerless in the face of a fathomless universe. I don't know about you, but the mind-set required for full throttle determinism makes it difficult for me to get out of bed. You've got to feel choice in order to survive, even if choice isn't real.

W.B. Yeats, in his years as a member of the occult secret society Order Of the Golden Dawn, describes my predicament perfectly when he says:

> For all men, certainly all imaginative men, must

> be for ever casting forth enchantments, glamours, illusions; and all men, especially tranquil men who have no powerful egotistic life, must be continually passing under their power.

I like that. Better to draft your own delusions than fall prey to the delusions of others. Given the endless variety of interpretations available to us, why not choose to see subtle energies at play? Why not behave as if we are the bosses of those energies? What's a writer anyway, but someone who goes about convinced, at least a little bit, of her own divinity?

Yeats, like me, had a complex relationship with his native Protestantism, a love life of trial and error, and a wide streak of spiritual dilettantism. Unlike me, he was also a genius, and his esoteric leanings deeply informed his work. It's hard to imagine any of his poetry without the whimsy and grandeur of his kooky theories. It's what gives us the creeps in "The Second Coming." Remember that "rough beast" with the human head and the lion's body, slouching through the desert where Aleister Crowley performed arcane gay sex rituals—on his honeymoon?

An aside: Wives were unimaginably tolerant at this time. Yeats's wife, twenty-five years his junior—whose automatic writing inspired many of his later poems—let him get his other needs met all over town.

I DRAW the Devil. He's a big charming goat with two pet humans, chains looped gently around their necks. I am stuck in a loop with work, and desperate to get out of it. Is this Commitment or Addiction? Loyalty or Ambivalence? I can't tell if I need more stubborn conviction or more fearlessness. I do know I tend to suffer longer than necessary to figure things out, but the Devil says maybe I like it. This predicts nothing, but shows me what I already know, which comforts me.

Even the cleverest of us need magical thinking to tolerate all the "mere anarchy loosed upon the world." Some drink and grow bitter or ruin the lives of their wives. Some spend years lost in ancient Hindu texts or look to architecture for spiritual guidance. I'm apt to give myself a hard time about this, as if I should suffer materialism nobly, be one of those best that "lack all conviction" but I have a long to-do list and a short fuse, and people depend on me to ameliorate the hell out of my obsessions. I make a poor atheist. Physicists and mathematicians say we live in an improbable world, that all these atoms smashing about, making consciousness, more likely originate from a computer simulation than from the sky and sea and dirt our senses perceive. As an allegory, the computer simulation lacks charm, but I understand the impulse. Whatever meaning machine you spend your life staring at will eventually begin to look like God. Even cards. Even words.

Acknowledgments

Thank you to my family and friends who tolerate appearing in print without opportunity for rebuttal. Thank you to my husband and kiddos, Patrick, Sully and Hank, for loving me and supporting me and reading my rough drafts. Thank you to all of the Propeller Books team, and Dan DeWeese in particular. Without his gentle but persistent pestering, the essays in this book would not exist, and without his devotion to small press publishing the rest of it wouldn't, either.

Bibliography

sources for lines found in this book

p. 1: "I too, dislike it"
Moore, Marianne. "Poetry." *Others for 1919: An Anthology of the New Verse*. London: Forgotten Books, 2017.
p. 5: "Tamed by Miltown, we lie on Mother's bed."
Lowell, Robert. "Man and Wife." *Life Studies and for the Union Dead*. New York: Farrar, Straus and Giroux, 2007.
p. 9: "When I had no mother, I embraced order."
Pinsky, Robert. "Samurai Song." *Jersey Rain*. New York: Farrar, Straus and Giroux, 2001.
p. 13: "That which is given to see"
Ashbery, John. "The Gazing Grain." *Houseboat Days*. New York: Penguin, 1977.
p. 17: "Perfume is what the flowers throw away."
Valery, Paul. "Of Colors." *Collected Works of Paul Valery, Vol 2: Poems in the Rough*. Princeton University Press, 1970.
p. 19: "It is a turbid, muddled, gothic sort of an affair..."
James, William. *William James: Writings 1902-1910*. Library of America, 1988.
p. 25: "Death is no different whined at than withstood."
Larkin, Philip. "Aubade." *Collected Poems*. New York: Farrar, Straus and Giroux, 2004.
p. 29: "*An outbreak of severalness...*"
Young, Dean. "House of Geodes." *Embryoyo*. Las Vegas: Believer Books, 2007.
p. 29: "Literal meanings are packaged commodities..."
Brown, Norman O. *Love's Body*. Berkeley: University of California Press, 1966.

p. 33: "I meant behavior is a pile of clothes"
Armantrout, Rae. "Life's Work." *Partly: New and Selected Poems, 2001–2015*. Indiana: Wesleyan, 2017.
p. 37: "This is not an age of beauty"
Phillips, Emilia. "Age of Beauty." *Poem-a-Day*. The Academy of American Poets, January 3, 2017.
p. 41 "All we can say in the face of our insane..."
Ruefle, Mary. "On Sentimentality." *Madness, Rack, and Honey*. Seattle: Wave Books, 2012.
p. 45: "To see you again, isn't love revision?"
Shaughnessy, Brenda. "One Love Story, Eight Takes." *Human Dark with Sugar*. Port Townsend: Copper Canyon Press, 2008.
p. 49: "O didn't you know I'd been ruined, said she."
Hardy, Thomas. "The Ruined Maid." *The Collected Poems of Thomas Hardy*. England: Wordsworth Editions, 1994.
p. 55: "She casts her best, she flings herself..."
Patmore, Coventry. *Angel in the House*. Ulan Press, 2012.
p. 59: "You have to improve your portrait of God"
Ashbery, John. "We Hesitate." *Shadow Train*. New York: Penguin, 1981.
p. 63: "Huffy Henry hid the day"
Berryman, John. "Dream Song 1." *The Dream Songs*. New York: Farrar, Straus and Girous, 2014.
p. 67: "a pause a little emptiness"
Arnold, Craig. "Meditation on a Grapefruit." *Poetry* October 2009.
p. 71: "For all men, certainly all imaginative men..."
Yeats, W.B. "Ideas of Good and Evil." *Essays and Introductions*. New York: Macmillan, 1961.

www.ingramcontent.com/pod-product-compliance
Lightning Source LLC
Chambersburg PA
CBHW031359060726
47590CB00007B/2853

* 9 7 8 0 9 8 2 7 7 0 4 7 4 *